THIS IS

Put your name here

WORK

On-the-job learning

© 2015 by Jennifer Kuiper
Title: This is your work
Subtitle: On-the-job learning
Author: Jennifer Kuiper

ISBN-13: 978-1514837474
ISBN-10: 1514837471

Publisher: Jen B.V. Zaandam – The Netherlands
Website: www.thisisyourworkbook.com
Design & illustrations: Mr.Prezident
Editor: Gina Wisse, Het Boekenschap

On-the-job learning: learning from the tasks or
activities you engage in as part of your work.

WRITE DOWN YOUR NAME ON THE COVER OF THIS BOOK.

Keep this book strictly confidential,
so that you can use it to write,
glue and draw whatever you want.

This book provides practical exercises and insights for learning from the tasks or activities you engage in as part of your work.

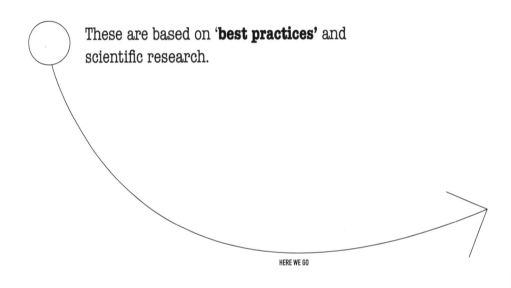

These are based on '**best practices**' and scientific research.

HERE WE GO

Did you know that most learning occurs in day-to-day work and not in the classroom?

Tick the **correct** answer:*

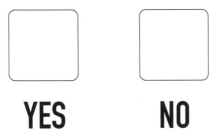

YES   NO

* You have answered correctly

Remember that there are no rules, that you can take notes any time you want to, and that there are no rights and wrongs.

Pick a relevant exercise from this book at regular intervals, such as every day or every week. **The sequence is not important.**

FOLLOW THE INSTRUCTIONS ON THE PAGES.

To use this book to its **full** potential, you need a couple of items. **Tick** any items you do not have yet. Then, **tear** out this page if you need a shopping list.

Supplies:

○ **PEN OR PENCIL**
○ **FELT-TIP PENS OR COLOURED CRAYONS**
○ **TAPE OR STAPLES**
○ **INTERNET ACCESS**

When you're done, **tape** this page back into your book to keep it complete.

SHOPPING LIST

HOW CAN EFFECTIVE ON-

Cross out the statements that
are not applicable to
your situation.

Make my day-to-day work more challenging

Improve my performance

Keep up with change

Increase my chances to get promotion or a higher salary

Enjoy my day-to-day work more

Set on-the-job learning goals and targets

Be a more effective learner

Identify the most valuable on-the-job learning opportunities

THE-JOB LEARNING AND THIS BOOK HELP YOU?

Learn more from colleagues and extend my personal learning network

Reflect on learning experiences more and apply the learned lessons to current and future work

Use my time effectively

Boost the results of learning from my day-to-day activities

Other:

Written and unwritten rules will vary per workplace.

If you doubt whether an exercise is acceptable in your workplace, you have some choices.

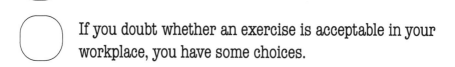

MY TIP! IF YOU THINK YOU WILL END UP REGRETTING DOING A CERTAIN EXERCISE, DO NOT DO IT. It is your own responsibility to make the right choices.

Please **tick** your preferred choice:

○ Leave out the exercise

○ Discuss the situation with a colleague or manager

○ Try it anyway and take full responsibility for what happens

We all have different comfort levels with respect to the challenges and work pressure we can handle.
Make sure you stay within your own limits.

START
HERE

Three instances from my work history when
I learned a lot in a short space of time:

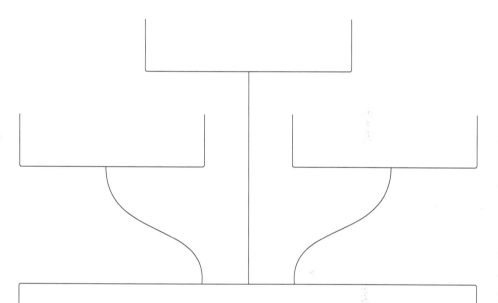

What did these instances have in common?

On-the-job learning happens everywhere and in all kinds of ways.

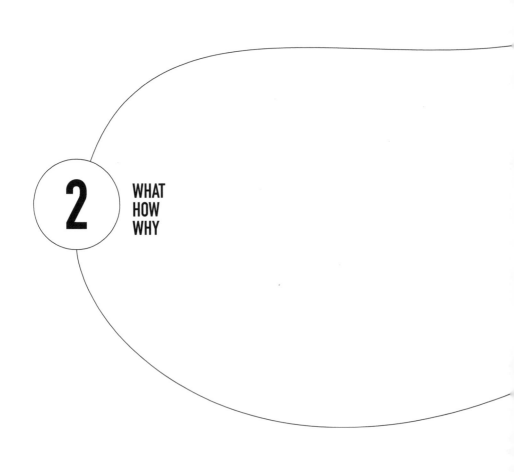

2 WHAT
HOW
WHY

Write down three things that you have learned on the job
in the past month.

**WHAT
HOW
WHY**

**WHAT
HOW
WHY**

On these pages, create a coloured stain that
expresses how you feel about on-the-job learning.

Find a colleague with whom you can discuss a challenging
activity you need to carry out. Use this conversation to
clarify and fine-tune your own ideas.
Write down the best idea here.

Getting new insights into your preferred way of on-the-job learning

☐ OBSERVATION I like to observe others. I analyse what I find useful and then apply this to my own work.

☐ EXCHANGING IDEAS I talk, discuss or brainstorm with others. Their reactions and ideas inspire me during my learning process.

☐ GATHERING KNOWLEDGE There is a high chance you will find me with my face buried in a book. I enjoy learning from experts who share their knowledge.

MY SOURCE RUIJTERS, M. (2006). LIEFDE VOOR LEREN. Deventer: Kluwer.

Tick your favourite way(s) of learning.

☐ **PRACTISING** I enjoy learning in an environment that is simple and safe enough for mistakes to be made. By making mistakes, I learn everything I need to know. I need someone to guide me, to simplify situations and to point things out to me. Repetition is important to me.

☐ **EXPLORING** I learn by jumping in at the deep end. Curiosity, coincidence, creativity and self-control guide me through the learning process. You are unlikely to find me in a formal learning environment such as a course or workshop, because these methods are too limiting and static for me.

THIS IS WHAT I WANT TO LEARN:

Use these boxes to write down three things you want to learn and explain why.

Cut out the boxes and paste them onto the next page in order of priority.

THIS IS WHAT I WANT TO LEARN:

This is what I want to learn:

A DIFFICULT SITUATION ...

MY CURRENT KNOWLEDGE/SKILLS/ BEHAVIOUR ...

NEW KNOWLEDGE/SKILLS/BEHAVIOUR I COULD USE IN THIS SITUATION ...

MY SOURCE — DE GALAN, K. (2007). TRAININGEN ONTWERPEN. PEARSON EDUCATION.

NEGATIVE RESULT ...

EXPECTED POSITIVE RESULT ...

NOTES

On this page, write down why and how you want to learn from your day-to-day activities.

NAME:

WHAT I WANT TO LEARN:

WHY I WANT TO LEARN THIS:

THE STEPS I AM GOING TO TAKE:

Tear out this page and put it on your office wall in a highly visible place. Mark the actions you have completed.

WHAT HAS CHALLENGED ME TODAY:

WHAT I WOULD DO DIFFERENTLY NEXT TIME:

WHAT I HAVE LEARNED FROM THIS:

FUTURE SITUATIONS IN WHICH I CAN APPLY WHAT I HAVE LEARNED TODAY:

Make a Scoop.it!

Networking = the art of sharing ideas, knowledge, expertise, stories and values with others, based on a common professional interest.

TODAY, SPEND AT LEAST TEN MINUTES EXTENDING OR MAINTAINING YOUR PERSONAL LEARNING NETWORK.

Note down your activities and results in the bubbles below and give each of them a colour that matches your feelings.

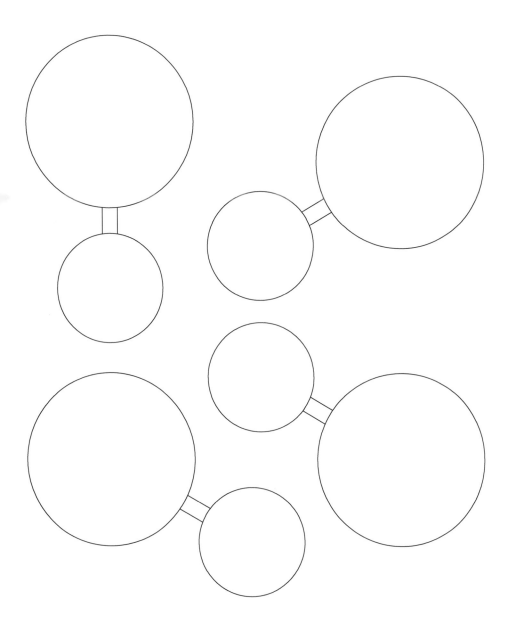

A new challenge?
Note down the following.

WHAT I ALREADY KNOW ABOUT THE SUBJECT:

THE SKILLS I NEED AND ALREADY POSSESS:

RELEVANT ACTIONS I HAVE CARRIED OUT BEFORE:

MY CONCLUSION

☐ This is more than I expected.
☐ This is less than I expected.

My favourite way of on-the-job learning

How I can apply my favourite way of on-the-job learning to my workplace

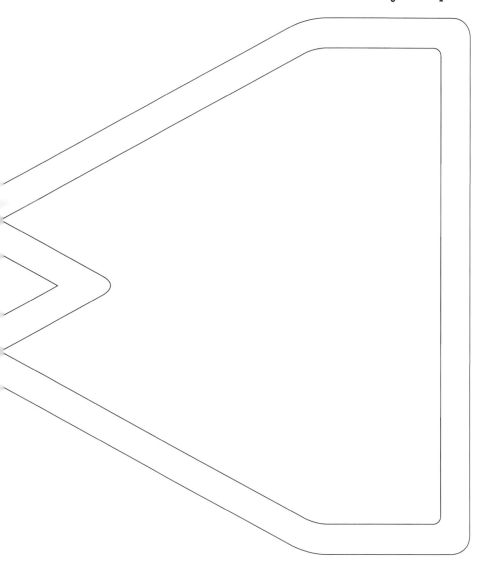

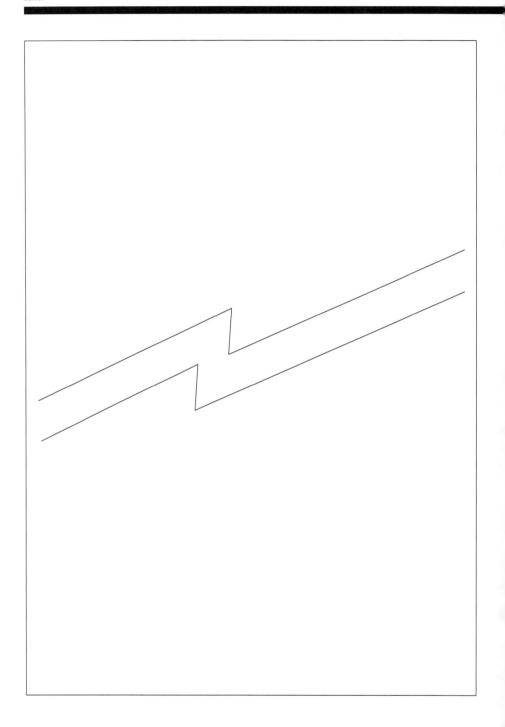

Today, find a colleague who is very skilled at something you would like to learn.

For at least **one hour**, imitate him or her as accurately as possible. Make sure nobody notices.

Afterwards, **write down** what you have learned from this exercise while copying the handwriting of your colleague as closely as possible.

WHAT IS YOUR GOAL?

WHERE ARE YOU NOW?

WHAT IS YOUR NEXT STEP?

A new challenge

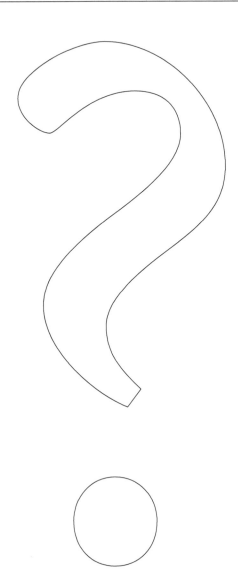

What are the similarities and differences with activities you have carried out in the past?

SIMILARITIES

DIFFERENCES

A SET-
BACK

What have I learned from this?

What would I do differently next time?

In which future situations can I apply what I have learned from this?

Divide the skill you want to learn into sub-skills.

WRITE THEM DOWN ON THE NEXT PAGE.

The skill I want to learn:

....

The sub-skills:

Cut out the sub-skills and put them in order of when you will be practising them. Then glue them onto the next page of this book.

MY TIP — READ THE FIRST 20 HOURS. HOW TO LEARN ANYTHING... FAST! BY JOSH KAUFMAN (2013). Penguin: New York OR WATCH HIS TEDX-VIDEO ON YOUTUBE.

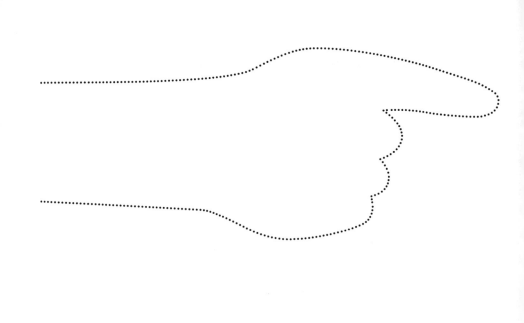

The order in which I will be practising the sub-skills: SEE PREVIOUS PAGE.

A MEETING WITH YOUR MOST DIFFICULT CLIENT

What went well (congratulations!)?

What went less well?

Ask a colleague for advice on how to do better next time.
Write down the advice below as a resolution for yourself.

Take a pen or felt-tip pen and scribble below until you have re-
leased all your frustration.

Mind map

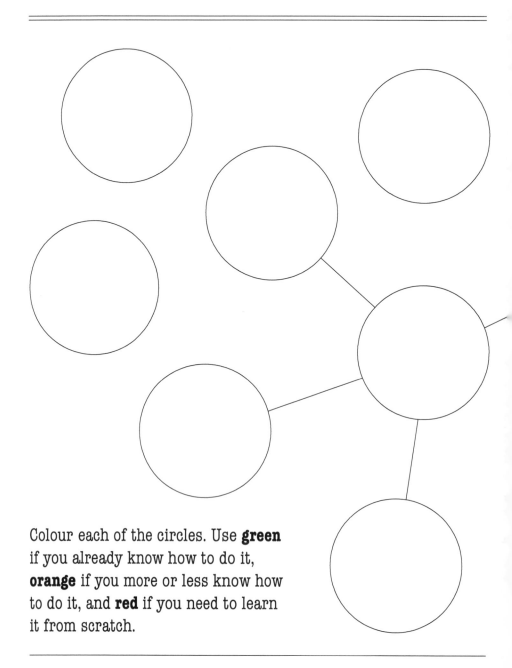

Colour each of the circles. Use **green** if you already know how to do it, **orange** if you more or less know how to do it, and **red** if you need to learn it from scratch.

Create a mind map showing all the skills you need in order to do your job well or to prepare yourself for a next step in your career.

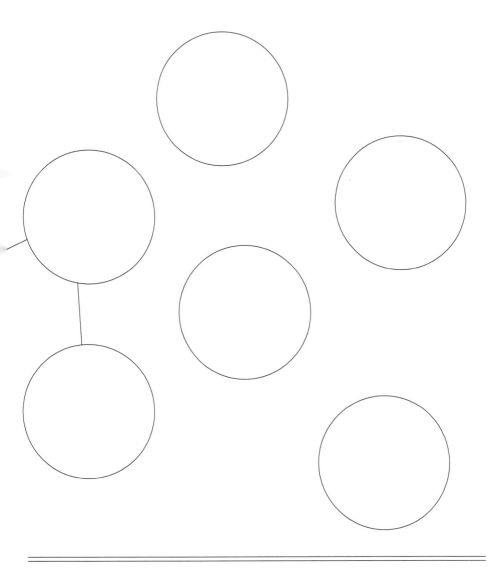

Have you learned anything that you would like to use again in the near future?

Turn this page into a crib sheet. Write down any useful tips and tricks.

Fold down the top right-hand corner of this page so you can easily find it back.

Look for a practical model or relevant tips for your learning goal.

Use learning materials from your corporate university, **Mindtools.com**, **Lynda.com** (practical, short courses for a reasonable price) or **Coursera.org** (a lot are free of charge and developed by reputable universities).

You can also look for information on other websites.

Summarise the practical model or relevant tips below.

Time for a **test!** Apply the model to your situation straight away and make a note of your results on the first empty page you can find.

Study the working methods of people around you and describe what makes their way of working **effective** or **ineffective** below.

Study your own working methods and describe what
makes your way of working **effective** or **ineffective**
below.

Cut out the box below and give it to a colleague prior to a meeting.

AFTER THIS MEETING, WOULD YOU PLEASE GIVE ME FEED-BACK ON [   ]?

- What went well?

- What did not go well and why?

- What can I do differently next time?

Notes

WHAT IS THE BIGGEST PROBLEM IN THE DEPART-MENT OR ORGANISATION YOU WORK AT? WHAT HAS BEEN BOTHERING EVERYONE FOR A LONG TIME?

Take the **initiative** and responsibility for solving this.

- Afterwards, write down what you have learned from this.

- Give yourself a treat when you have finished.

- Draw this on the page on the right.

What is the biggest mistake you have made at work?

In six to eight sentences, describe what you did and what you would do if you had the chance to relive that experience.

Steps I will take to reach my on-the-job learning goal:

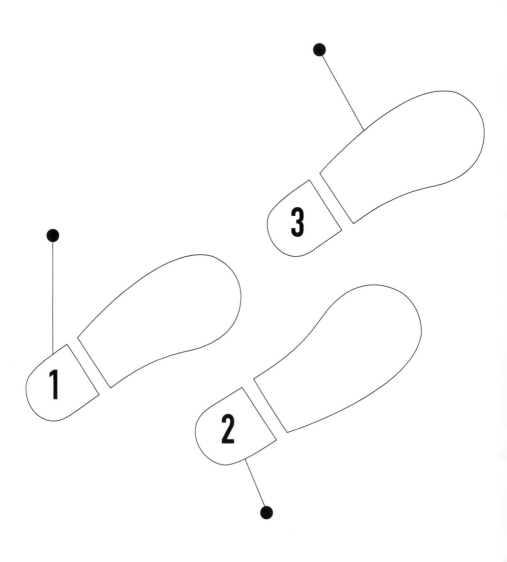

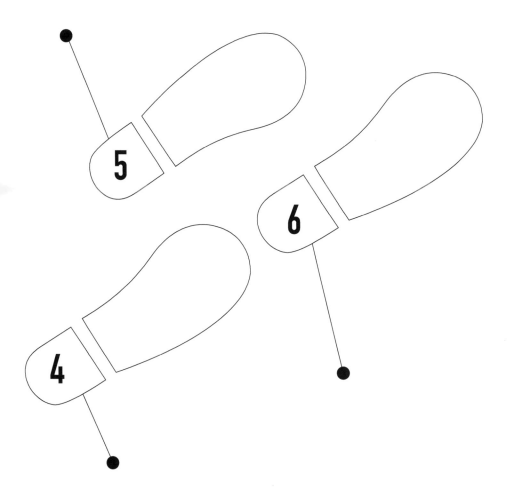

Did you learn what you wanted to learn?
Describe the results in words, make a drawing or use a picture.

Find at least three books, articles, YouTube videos, SlideShare files or other specific training materials about the subject you want to learn about.

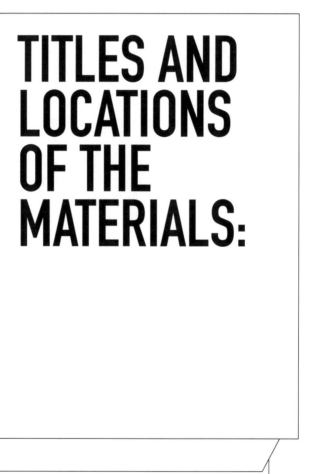

TITLES AND LOCATIONS OF THE MATERIALS:

1

2

3

Secure a place for yourself in a multi-disciplinary team in your organisation. This team should be assigned to either solve a problem or to develop something new.

Name:

Name:

What I would like to learn from this colleague:

What I would like to learn from this colleague:

Below, draw the portraits of the team members who you think you could learn most from. Below each portrait, note down what you would like to learn from that particular colleague.

Name:

Name:

What I would like to learn from this colleague:

What I would like to learn from this colleague:

In mirror writing, write down what you have actually learned from these four team members and how you are planning to apply this knowledge.

In mirror writing, write down what you have actually learned from these four team members and how you are planning to apply this knowledge.

Afterwards, try to read your text in front of a mirror to see if it makes sense.

HAVE YOU LEARNED ANYTHING THAT YOU WOULD LIKE TO USE AGAIN IN THE NEAR FUTURE?

!! EXPLAIN HOW YOU WOULD DO THIS STEP BY STEP !!

Then fold down the top right-hand corner
of this page so you can easily find these
instructions back.

Fill in the postcard below, cut it out and put it in an envelope.
Keep the envelope in your cupboard or your drawer. Wait sixty
days and then send the envelope to yourself.

WHAT I AM GOING TO LEARN FROM MY DAY-TO-DAY WORK:

WHY I WANT TO LEARN THIS:

MY PLAN OF APPROACH:

WHAT I WILL HAVE ACCOMPLISHED IN TWO MONTHS' TIME:

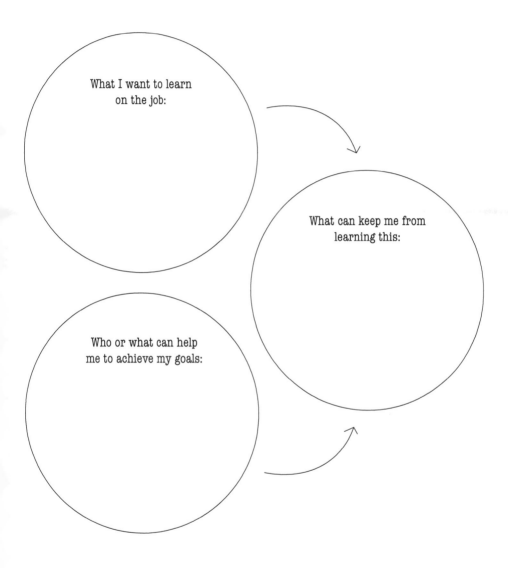

What I want to learn
on the job:

What can keep me from
learning this:

Who or what can help
me to achieve my goals:

TICK OFF THE OPPORTUNITIES YOU WILL NOT MISS OUT ON:

○ Replacing my manager during holiday or sick leave

○ Taking over work from my manager when he or she is overloaded

○ Taking my manager's place in a meeting, for example when he or she has been double-booked

○ Other:

_____

_____

_____

_____

_____

_____

_____

Notes

Open your diary. For every working day, reserve ten minutes to maintain and extend your personal learning network.

A difficult task. Ask someone in your network for help.

Request:

Support that I received:

FIND A QUIET PLACE, CLOSE YOUR EYES AND VISUALIZE A FUTURE CHALLENGE AT WORK STEP BY STEP.

TWO SHORT SUCCESS STORIES:

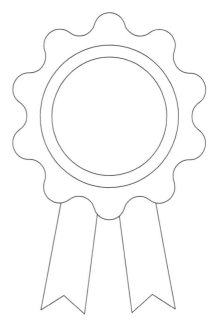

FEEDBACK

Circle your usual reaction to any feedback you receive:

I take this personally and reject what is said by:

> Twisting the meaning
>
> Denying
>
> Attacking
>
> Withdrawing

$\longrightarrow$

Resistance to change:

> No learning
>
> No insights
>
> No improvement

I deal with this professionally and start working on it by:

> Analysing
>
> Discussing
>
> Clarifying
>
> Understanding

$\longrightarrow$

Applying change:

> Learning new things
>
> New insights
>
> Improvement

$\longrightarrow$ Defensive behaviour; keeps your colleagues from giving you feedback again.

$\longrightarrow$ Gratitude for openness and honesty from others; leads to satisfaction and further development.

Below, draw or make a note of the most important resources you have for on-the-job learning.

Then, underneath each circle, write down how you will use the resource to reach your learning goals.

TRY
SOMETHING
NEW
TODAY!

WRITE AN ARTICLE FOR YOUR FAVOURITE MAGAZINE.

THE ARTICLE MUST CONTAIN AT LEAST:

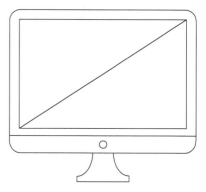

- one new thing you have learned on the job;
- how you learned this;
- what contributed most and least to your learning;
- an explanation of how you will apply this knowledge in the future.

 SHARE THIS ARTICLE WITH AT LEAST THREE PEOPLE.

Finish the article by adding a photo that illustrates an important element of your article.

Write a draft version of your article below.

Write a blog post every week for three weeks.

YOUR BLOG SHOULD AT LEAST CONTAIN:

- What you have learned on the job during the past week;
- Your highs and lows;
- What you are looking forward to next week;
- An invitation for others to comment on your blog.

 SHARE YOUR BLOG WITH AT LEAST THREE PEOPLE.

MY TIP WHICH TOOLS ARE AVAILABLE AT YOUR COMPANY? FREE ONLINE TOOLS ARE WWW.BLOGGER.COM AND WWW.WORDPRESS.COM.
BE CAREFUL WHEN SELECTING THE INFORMATION YOU SHARE ON YOUR BLOG. WHEN IN DOUBT, ASK YOUR MANAGER FOR ADVICE OR PERMISSION.

Design your own on-the-job learning exercise. Write it down below and then do the exercise yourself.

Do you want to share your on-the-job learning exercise and receive feedback? Send it to thisisyourwork @gmail.com.

How are you getting on with your on-the-job learning? Circle the
emoticon that shows how you feel about this in the best way.

◯ Write down what you want to learn.

Describe in as much detail as possible what others will notice and experience when you have reached your goal. ◯

Today, ask at least three people close to you about something you want to learn from the tasks or activities you engage in as part of your work. Write down the questions and answers on this page in three different fonts.

Question:

Answer:

Question:

Answer:

Question:

Answer:

FEEDBACK

Write down what you will change
based on this feedback.

Make a note of the
feedback you regularly
receive from people here.

Describe your first
action here.

USE A
BORING
MEETING OR
DISCUSSION
AS A LEARNING
OPPORTUNITY.

Observe the different communication styles used and write them down.

Which communication style works?

Which communication style works?

How can you prove this?

Which style does not seem to work?

How can you prove this?

How and when can you use the lessons you learned?

MY TIP — WOULD YOU LIKE TO LEARN MORE ABOUT COMMUNICATION STYLES BEFORE DOING THIS EXERCISE SO YOU HAVE A FRAME OF REFERENCE? SEARCH FOR INFORMATION ON THE INTERNET, REVIEW BEST PRACTICES (ON MINDTOOLS.COM, FOR EXAMPLE), OR SIGN UP FOR AN ONLINE COURSE (VIA YOUR CORPORATE UNIVERSITY OR ON LYNDA.COM, FOR INSTANCE).

 Interview an expert on the subject that you are trying to learn more about. Summarise your questions and the answers you received below.

In the form of a fairytale, tell the story of a learning experience you have had while carrying out your job.

Once upon a time there was a ....

....

....

....

....

....

....

....

....

....

....

....

....

....

....

....

....

.... and he/she lived happily ever after.

WHICH PEOPLE IN YOUR NETWORK GIVE YOU USEFUL ADVICE, NEW INSIGHTS AND FEEDBACK WITHOUT YOU HAVING TO ASK FOR IT?

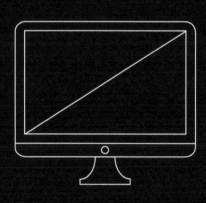

Ask one of these people to be your mentor for the next month(s).

STAYING ALERT

Ask your colleague if he/she wants to accept this 'invitation'.

Share what you would like to learn on the job with a colleague.

Explain why you want to learn this and how you are planning to approach this.

Ask your colleague to keep you alert by reminding you of your plan on a daily/weekly basis.

Promise you will take over a tedious task from him/her if you do not complete your plan successfully.

Today, check if you are on track to complete your on-the-job learning plan.

Colour the big plus sign **green** if you are on track or ahead of your schedule. Colour the big minus sign **red** if you are behind schedule.

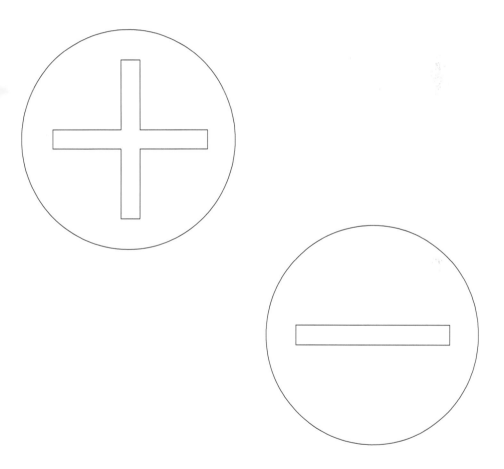

WAIT FOR THE RIGHT MOMENT.

Ask your manager if the two of you can arrange a regular meeting to discuss your professional development.

Draw or glue your self-portrait on here.

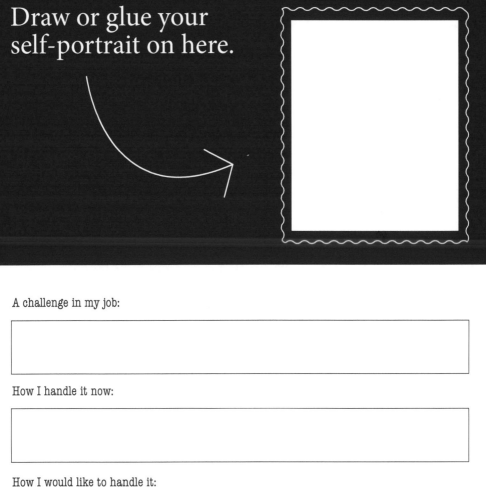

A challenge in my job:

How I handle it now:

How I would like to handle it:

How I am going to learn this:

RESEARCH THE SUBJECT THAT YOU ARE LEARNING ON THE JOB.

Which people are frequently discussed and quoted? Who has published a lot of articles on this subject? Write down their names. Which new insights have their publications given you and how can you apply this to your daily work?

Names, new insights and how to apply this:

Create practical work instructions for a challenging task in the form of an infographic.

Have you been following an (online) course that is relevant for your whole team? If so, share your most important findings with your colleagues.

Note down what you have learned from sharing your findings with your colleagues.

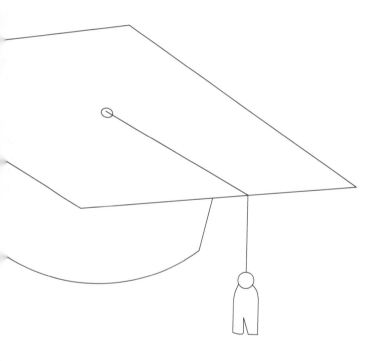

FOR AN (ONLINE) COURSE YOU HAVE FOLLOWED, APPLY THE NEW KNOWLEDGE OR SKILLS TO AN ACTIVITY YOU HAVE SCHEDULED FOR TODAY.

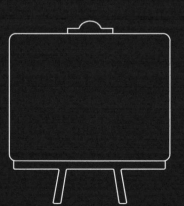

A challenging situation:

What I have learned from this:

What I would do differently next time:

Future situations to which I can apply what I have learned today:

BENCHMARK

Find the highest standard within the subject you want to learn on the job. Compare yourself to the highest standard.

Note down your findings and how you can further improve yourself below.

SPONTANEOUSLY CALL OR MESSAGE A COLLEAGUE OR SOMEONE IN YOUR NETWORK WHO HAS A SIMILAR JOB TO YOURS.

Invite yourself for a guided tour.

Suggest inviting a guest speaker to the next important staff meeting. Make preparations for the session together with the guest speaker.

Write down what you have learned from this below.

ASK FOR ANONY- MOUS ADVICE!

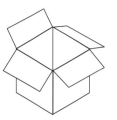

(1) Place an empty box with your name on it somewhere in the building – it must be out of your sight and in a safe place.

(2) Write down a concrete and open question about a specific situation on a piece of paper.

(3) Make at least four copies of this and hand them to colleagues who know you well. Ask them to give you anonymous advice.

(4) Inform these colleagues about the deadline for the advice and ask them to put their sheets into the box.

SHOW A NEW EMPLOYEE THE ROPES.

Write down the new insights that you gained:

WHAT ARE YOU LEARNING?

In the form of a story, describe what your working day will be like when you have mastered what you are currently learning.

MY ALARM GOES OFF EARLY...

Have you carried out the plan you made for on-the-job learning?

Answer the following questions:

What worked well?

What steps did not work well and why?

What will I do differently for my next goal?

Was the goal too difficult or too easy?

How do I feel now that I have reached my goal?

[ ]

Is this what I really wanted?

[ ]

Should my next goal be easier or harder, or take shorter or longer to reach? Should it fit into my everyday life better?

[ ]

Are more, less or different kinds of resources and support necessary for me to reach my next goal?

[ ]

WHILE KEEPING
IN MIND YOUR
ON-THE-JOB
LEARNING GOALS,
MAKE AT LEAST ONE
NEW CONTACT TODAY.

 Write down how you are going to maintain and extend your personal learning network below.

TALK TO A COLLEAGUE AND AGREE TO COACH EACH OTHER.

Discuss why and how you will do this.

My coaching question:

My colleague's coaching question:

How:

 MY TIP   IF NECESSARY, LOOK UP THE BEST WAYS TO COACH EACH OTHER ON THE INTERNET AND STUDY EXAMPLES OF WELL-STATED COACHING QUESTIONS.

QUESTION FOR

Write down the name here
or draw the portrait

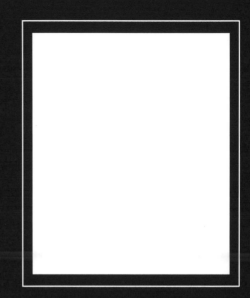

How did you do that?

How did you learn that?

Could you teach me how to do that too?

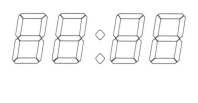

At a regular time at the end of the day (e.g. on your way home from work), get into the habit of asking yourself the following.

What went well, what did not go well and why?

What have I learned today?

MY TIP FIND A SPOT THAT CATCHES THE EYE AND PUT DOWN A NOTE THAT HELPS YOU TO REMEMBER THIS ROUTINE EVERY DAY.

What could I do better or differently tomorrow?

How am I going to do this?

Come up with an improved way of carrying out an important activity.

Ask for the advice of at least **one** colleague.

ACTIVITY

Description of the improved method:

Share your knowledge or experience. Write a piece for a newsletter, wiki, blog or other medium. Let your manager or a more experienced colleague review this.
Make sure that it gets published.

Below, write down the reactions you received and any new contacts you gained from this experience.

Surprise yourself, your colleagues, your manager or a client.
Do something you are already very good at, even better.

What I am already good at:

How I can do this even better:

How I did this much better:

Reactions I have heard or received:

How I feel about this:

SET UP AN INTERVISION GROUP.

Topic to discuss: **doing** your daily work and any challenges or problems you encounter

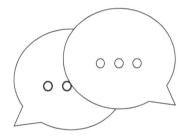

SEARCH FOR INFORMATION ABOUT THE INTERVISION METHOD
AND HOW YOU CAN MAKE THIS WORK ON THE INTERNET.

Two things I have learned this week:

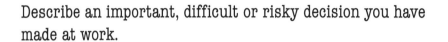

Describe an important, difficult or risky decision you have made at work.

What went well?

What would you rather have done differently?

What is the most important lesson you have learned from this?

Offer your support to a colleague who is having a hard time. Make a rhyme about what you learned from this.

THE BEST THING I HAVE LEARNED ON THE JOB THIS MONTH!

Describe it, draw it or use a picture to show it.

DARE!

Ask someone you trust and find competent to name your main improvement areas.

Ask what he/she thinks you should do to develop yourself more. Write down the answers on this page.

Observe your most successful colleague for as long as necessary in order to collect all the information you need.
Then write down:

Specific knowledge and insights that this colleague has:

Special skills that this colleague possesses:

The particular way in which this colleague behaves and the effect that this has:

The composition of the network that this colleague has built:

The traits I definitely do not want to take over:

TWO THINGS IN THE RECENT PAST THAT HAVE KEPT ME FROM....

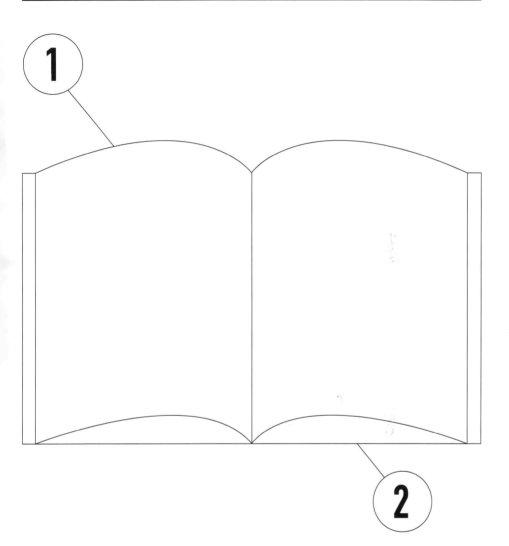

LEARNING SOMETHING:

ASK

Glue a photo onto this page or draw a portrait of the person that will help you with this exercise.

to show you how to approach .... (name a challenge you are facing). Take on the role of a witness. Write down what you have seen.

Describe or draw the obstacles that prevent you from on-the-job learning and add how you can work around these obstacles.

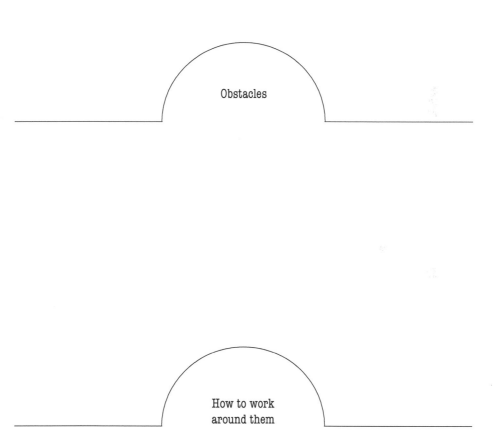

Obstacles

How to work
around them

Draw five circles of different sizes on this page.
In these circles, write down five things you have
learned on the job.

What have you discovered about yourself in relation to on-the-job learning in the past few weeks?

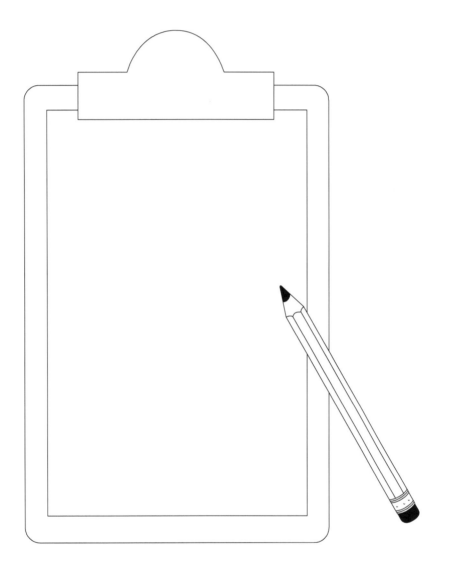

A QUICK CHECK ON HOW I AM DOING.

What I planned to learn on the job and when
I planned to finish:

Successes:

Obstacles:

Next steps:

The support I need:

BEGINNING OF THE DAY

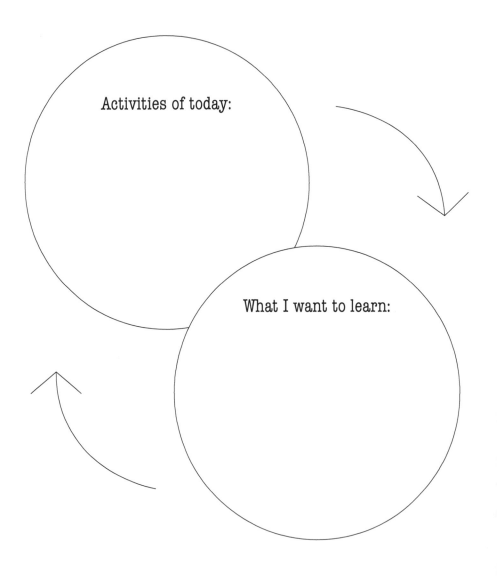

Activities of today:

What I want to learn:

END OF THE DAY

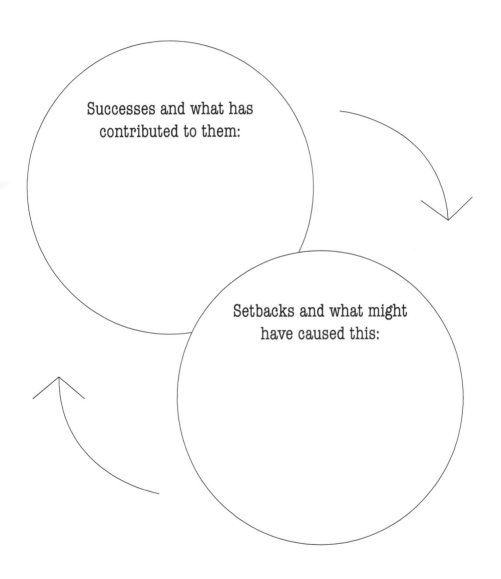

Successes and what has contributed to them:

Setbacks and what might have caused this:

ORGANISE A TRAINING SESSION, BITE–SIZED EVENT OR WORKSHOP:

1 INTERNALLY FOR COLLEAGUES FROM YOUR OWN OR OTHER DEPARTMENTS;

2 FOR VOLUNTEERS FOR A GOOD CAUSE IN THE COMMUNITY;

3 FOR A PROFESSIONAL (EDUCATIONAL) COURSE;

4 THROUGH A TRAINING INSTITUTE;

5 AND MANY MORE OPTIONS.

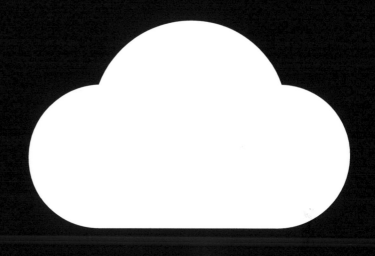

WHAT WOULD YOU LIKE TO BE REALLY GOOD AT?

WHAT CHALLENGES ME IN MY WORK:

Find an assignment or task that is more difficult than what you are used to. Determine what you want to learn from this before carrying it out.

Within my comfort zone

Out of my comfort zone

This week, find someone from outside your own department or location to work with.
Write down what you have learned from this below.

TAKE PART IN A PROJECT.

Find out which projects are about to start within your organisation. Write them down in the matrix below.

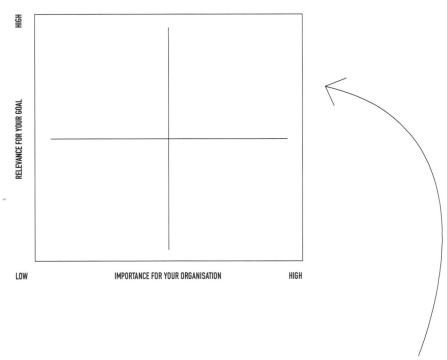

Choose the most valuable project.
Decide who is the best person to help you to get the role you want to fulfil.

DEVELOP, TEST OR IMPLEMENT A NEW PROCESS, SYSTEM OR PROCEDURE.

Is there a new process, system or procedure that needs to be developed, tested or implemented? Write them down in the matrix below.

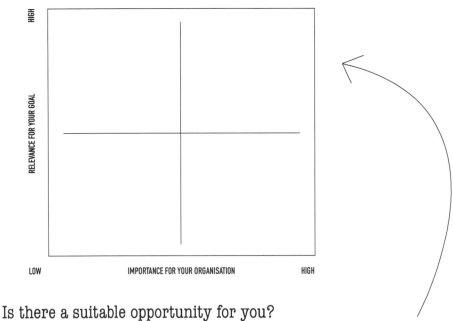

Is there a suitable opportunity for you?
If so, decide who would be the best person to help you to get the role you want to fulfil. Ask this person to help you.

REPRESENT YOUR TEAM, DEPARTMENT OR ORGANISATION.

Is there an opportunity to represent your team, department or organisation during a conference, senior management meeting or in another department? Write down the opportunities in the matrix below.

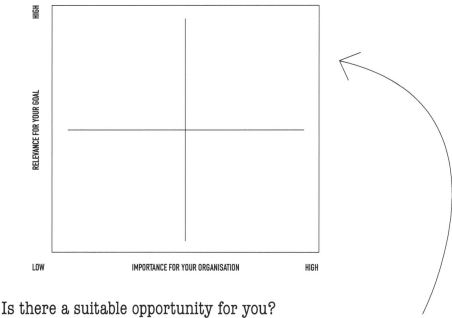

Is there a suitable opportunity for you?
If so, decide who would be the best person to help you to get the role you want to fulfil. Ask this person to help you.

FOCUS

Behind each box, write down a learning goal. Then number the boxes from 1 to 4.

1 = Very serious consequences if I do not know or cannot do this.

2 = Serious consequences if I do not know or cannot do this.

3 = Limited consequences if I do not know or cannot do this.

4 = Very limited consequences if I do not know or cannot do this.

☐

☐

☐

☐

Focus your attention on learning goals and activities labelled with a 1 or a 2.

TODAY, TEACH AT LEAST ONE COLLEAGUE SOMETHING YOU KNOW HOW TO DO REALLY WELL!

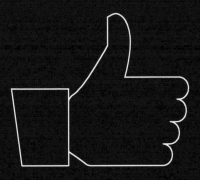

INCREASE THE SCOPE OF YOUR RESPONSIBILITIES.

Are there any activities that you can engage in, that increase the scope of your responsibilities? Write down the activities in the matrix below.

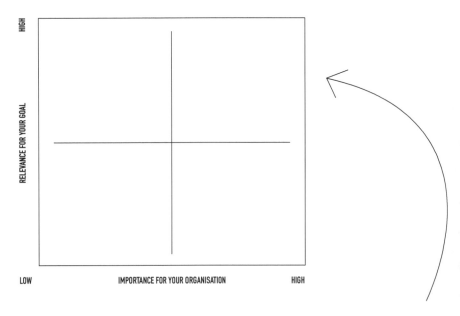

Is there a suitable opportunity for you?
If so, decide who would be the best person to help you to get the responsibility you want to have. Ask this person to help you.

WHAT HAVE YOU LEARNED IN THE PAST WEEK?

Is there something you will pay more attention to next time? Would you act in the same way again in a similar situation?

Make a note of your answers below or make a word cloud on www.wordle.net. Print this off and glue it into your book.

 Help a colleague with a big challenge or a difficult situation. Write down what you have learned from this.

TAKE OVER A TASK FROM YOUR MANAGER.

Find out which tasks you could take over from your manager.
Write these down in the matrix below.

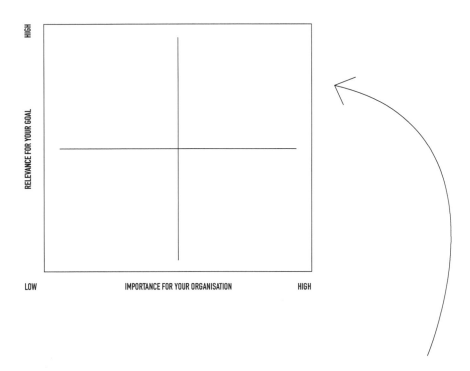

Is there a suitable opportunity for you?
If so, decide who would be the best person to help you to get
the role you want to fulfil. Ask this person to help you.

REPEAT A SKILL YOU HAVE JUST LEARNED AT LEAST THREE TIMES.

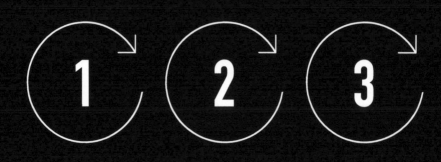

DID SOMETHING GO WRONG?

Do not worry about the consequences right now (there will be plenty of time to do this later), but learn from it!

What went wrong:	Reasons:

DESCRIBE OR VISUALIZE HOW THE SITUATION WOULD HAVE LOOKED IF IT HAD GONE WELL.

What would you have done differently?	What can you learn from this?

If possible, ask for advice from a colleague or manager.

GIVE A PRESENTATION DURING YOUR NEXT TEAM MEETING.

Make a note of possible subjects in the matrix below and choose one from the top right-hand corner.

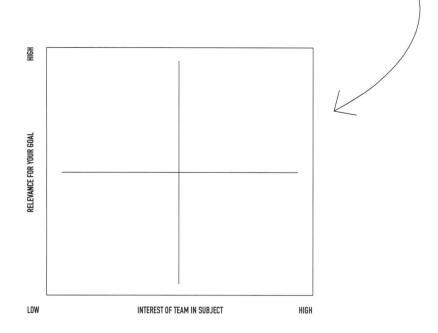

SHARE YOUR EXPERIENCE!

Are you enthusiastic about how you approached one of the exercises in this book or the results you achieved?

Please help others to explore the opportunities that learning from their day-to-day work can give them.

 SHARE YOUR SUCCESSES WITH OTHERS ON LINKEDIN, FACEBOOK, INSTAGRAM, SNAPCHAT, TWITTER, ETC.

SOLVE A PROBLEM OR A CRISIS.

Make an overview of all unsolved problems or perhaps, you can see a crisis coming your way. Write down the problems or crises in the matrix below.

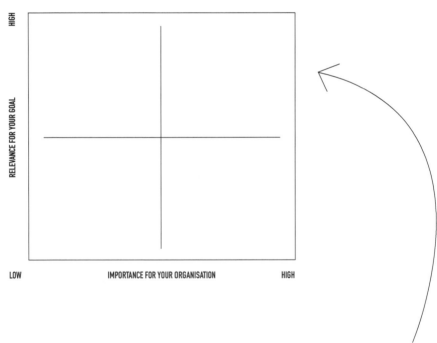

Is there a suitable opportunity for you? If so, decide who would be the best person to help you to get the role you want to fulfil. Ask this person to help you.

Design your own on-the-job learning exercise.
Write it down below and then carry it out.

Do you want to share your on-the-job learning exercise and
receive feedback? Send it to thisisyourwork@gmail.com

FEEDBACK

On-the-job learning and then sharing what I have learned with others is my passion. I would love to receive your feedback.

What did you like or enjoy about the book?

What did you not like about the book?

What should I definitely keep in the book?

Copy your text into an email, scan this page or take a picture of it and send this to: thisisyourwork@gmail.com.

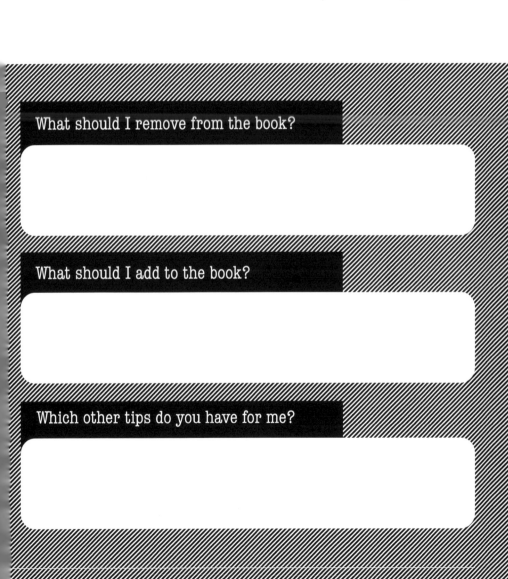

What should I remove from the book?

What should I add to the book?

Which other tips do you have for me?

Printed in Great Britain
by Amazon